The Awakening © 2023 Shy Brown

All rights reserved.

No part of this publication may be reproduced, stored in a retrieval system, or transmitted, in any form or by any means, electronic, mechanical, photocopying, recording, or otherwise, without the prior written permission of the presenters.

Shy Brown asserts the moral right to be identified as the author of this work.

Presentation by *BookLeaf Publishing*

Web: www.bookleafpub.com

E-mail: info@bookleafpub.com

ISBN: 9789357613750

First edition 2023

The Awakening

Shy Brown

BookLeaf Publishing

India | USA | UK

DEDICATION

Upbringing

Be careful of who you trust

Of whom you allow in your space

A close friend will try to steal

And even try to kill

All while trying to erase

Your destiny

Override your confidence with jealousy

Not your problem

Not your fault

That you were taught

To love God

Do right and correct your flaws

Character matters

Pride will lead to a straight-up downfall

Take out the trash

Do your best

It's still the work of the kingdom

Start from the bottom

Rise to the top

Humbleness you don't see in them

Feed others

Offer a meal

Love from the kitchen

This is what my parents taught me

From those Highway 45 trenches.

-To Clinton & Joyce Brown, thank you for raising me to be the best version of myself.

ACKNOWLEDGEMENT

Thank you for choosing to go on this journey with me.
It may be necessary for some and difficult for others.
My prayer for you is bravery and wisdom after turning each page.

PREFACE

Tell your story.
Share your truth.
You survived.

The Light

I Need Love

I need love that transcends
I need love that surpasses
All the words never said
A love that identifies my identity, my nature
A love that feeds my hunger and quenches my
thirst
I need love in every season
I need love for no reason
A love that encourages when doubtful
A love that comforts when lonely
I need love that can opt into every single desire
I need love that can put out no matter the hour
A love that understands my heart
A love that will never stop loving me, serving
me, raising me
All while passing on forces of atoms in a
spherical loop with no intention of stopping
This love is more than a want
It's more than a desire
It's a need to bless my nature, to balance my
soul
I don't feel whole
This is not typical
No time for performing rituals
Why? Because it's solely spiritual

No time for auditions
No time for sampling meals in the kitchen
I need love
Only the love that's for me
Only the one I should support to keep him from
going limp
I need love
Love needs me
Love's a need
One needs love
So, where's Love?

One Love

Physical, mental, natural appeal
Don't forget spiritual let's be real
People don't seem to be 'bout that life anymore
They rather sit still and not open the door
Of true sexual intimacy
The gift God gave for you to go into me
The idea of the Most High was romance
Nowadays we don't want to give it a chance
Because of all the scheming, cheating, and lies
I'm surprised to still hear of true love that hasn't
died
With all the love music that's ringing in our ears
You'd think there'd be lasting marriages of 30
plus years
Love we hear now is not the same
Too much scandal-ness, brokenness, deceit, and
pain
Where's the beauty, power, exclusiveness, and
ecstasy
Let me repeat, God's gift to us is sexual
intimacy
Intimacy that goes past physical features
Intimacy that goes beyond mind blowing teasers
This type of intimacy is tied to your soul, tied to
my soul

When you go into me, we are one whole
Fraction, doesn't matter who's the numerator or
denominator
We will always be One Love.

Small town, rural find
Rhyme time
Two kids' playtime
Yet finding time
To kiss and explore
Body parts, galore
First kiss shared
First best friend
First cherry popped trying to find
The beginning with no end
Then to separate, no more in sight
It just feels right
Relearning, reacquainting, wrestling
At first a struggle
Truth is the vision was bigger
Than the rebuttal
With dreams and visions greater
Than what the eyes can see
Looking back years later
Thank God that was me.

Precious Cargo

Precious cargo, I hold
Precious cargo, I've been entrusted with
Precious cargo, I didn't ask for
Hold up, wait a minute
I did!
Precious cargo, I've been gifted
Precious cargo, straight from the spirit
Precious cargo, beside me
Precious cargo, a reflection of me
Precious cargo, I don't want to live without
Precious cargo, at once a doubt
Precious cargo, I once fought
Precious cargo, I now sought
Precious cargo, I can't live without
Precious cargo, I never bought
Precious cargo, I must protect
Precious cargo, only I have the keys
Precious cargo, means so much to me
Precious cargo, may seem fragile
Precious cargo, I don't have to battle
Precious cargo, the love of my life
Precious cargo, I fell in love with you twice.

As much as I try to fight it
My feelings can't deny it
The way I feel about you inside
There's no need to hide it
I love you from the depth of my soul
That's deep for me
To truly say that and mean it
I'm starting to let go and I'm tired of fighting
You see
I didn't realize it until now
You've always held a special place in my heart
Memories of you and I
Laying a foundation from the start
Never in my wildest dreams
Would I have put this together
That's why our interaction can be nerve-wracking
and mind-boggling at times
I've wrestled with the idea and even with God
Now I just decided to step to the side
Let God have his way
This is all his doing and undoing
He's making old things new
You're here with me, I can see your transition too
My spirit is longing for your spirit
All this time it's been you
Give me your seed
And I'll give life back to you.

This is new, unfamiliar
But sort of familiar
At the same time peculiar
Exchange of words weaved into
A masterpiece of stories
Am I interested, or just here
To enjoy a rollercoaster of
Laughs, emotions, lessons learned
And even pain
Is this part of the plan
I can't stand the tests
And even the rain
Back and forth
But it's all part of the process.

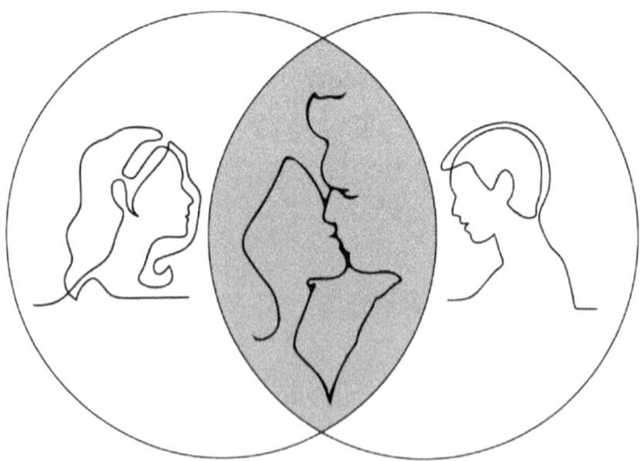

Who Holds the Key

Key to you
Key to me
Key to see
Where this can go
And what this can be
Quite skeptical in the natural
Yet kingdom in the spiritual
Never knew that God
Would bring this full circle
Had no idea this would be a ritual
Yet, I'm open to the possibilities
Not exactly what I had envisioned
For myself
It's not about what fits in my present
But rather kingdom building, top shelf
Your qualities gleam like silver armor
I see you for who you are
I embrace your becoming
Trajectory like a shooting star.

Lost in You

Good, bad, spiritual, sexual
How often do we allow ourselves to go
Deep in space, deep in sea with no point of
return
Not knowing when to come back
Or not even caring how to get back
It's like you've lost sight of land or your home
planet
In fact, you're happy you're lost
You're elated about not returning
Hell, you don't realize you're away from
Your home planet nor do you realize that
You've wandered away from grass and dirt
You're just out in space.
Space that you thought was open for you to
reside.
Space you thought was going to be your new
address.
Instead, the owner decided to vacate before you
even arrived.
Now you're lost.
Now you're naked.
In their eyes, you want to see home.

Perception, vibes, aura, energy
It's all affecting me
Messing up my emotions and creating
commotion within me
What I thought I once knew has been interrupted
By vocal opinions, stop messing with my
decisions
I thought I had it all together.
I thought I knew what I wanted.
It's all combobulated now, sometimes I think
I've been taunted.

Change or Stay the Same

The real against the fake
Why do I hate
To spread my wings and fly
Or should I
Just try to let go and soar
Against the grain
Which I do no more?
Could it be that I'm almost there?
Could it be that I'm right at the cuff of
impactful, mind-boggling change?
Change of body, the type of body I've always
wanted
Change of my environment
Seriously, what am I afraid of?
It's here.
It's now.
It's time to let go.
Be who God has called me to be.
No matter the obstacles.
No matter the find.
No water.
No deep.
No fish.
Cast your net.

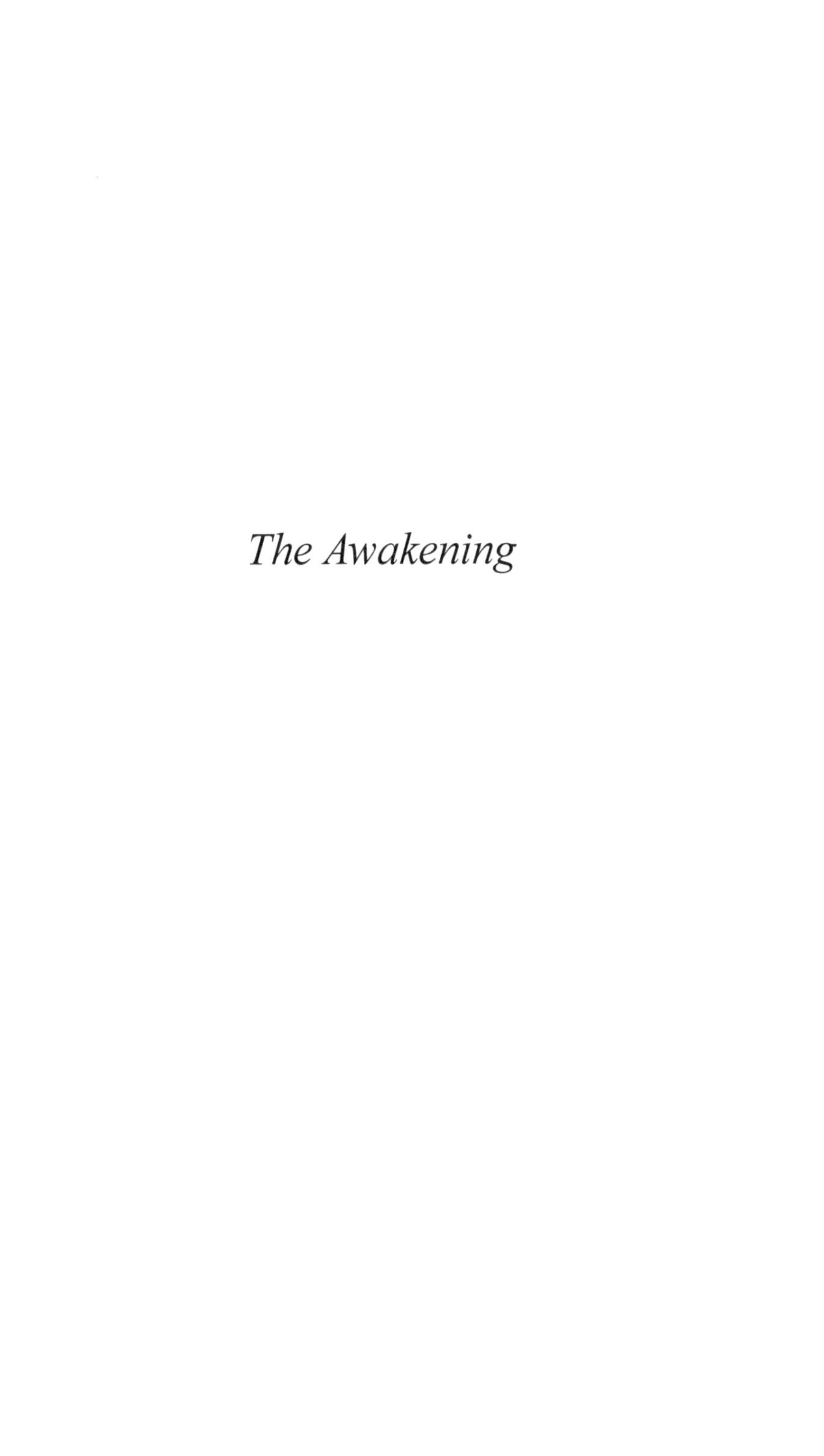

The Awakening

It Was All a Dream

What is life?
Is it a dream?
Is it a reality?
Is it a spiritual realization?
Or could it just be a figment of my imagination?

*-when you finally wake up, and wish it was all a
dream*

She Loves Him, She Loves Him Not

The more she wants to love him
The more she wants to walk away
The more she wants to hear his voice
The more she wishes she never answered his call
The more she wants to spend time with him
The more she wished she never laid eyes on him
She never understood a love/hate relationship
until now
Entries from her diary as a teen provided
evidence, or better yet insight, to what she
would experience as an adult with her first love.
By now she assumed old ways and habits would
have passed away to welcome a new human
being
But no, it was the total opposite
She was his first love. He was her first love.
They were kids.
She was his first kiss. He was her first kiss.
Again, they were kids.
If she placed a bet for one million dollars that
her first love wouldn't bring havoc into her life,
and cause her so much emotional pain and
trauma, she would have lost with no money to
spare.

From her experience, it was the worst relationship to ever be connected to.
From his experience, it was an escape from a previous life.
But why the different perceptions between the two?
Was it because of different expectations?
Was it because of different experiences?
Both had a past.
Hers was more grounded and with stability.
His was less stable with less ownership of responsibility.
She often wondered to herself why she chose to stay involved and waste her time.
Maybe it was the thought of a love story. Maybe she hoped things would get better. Maybe she was tired of being alone and wanted to try something new.
Thought after thought, feeling after feeling, emotion after emotion she experienced as she sat in a green open field scattered with sunflowers, poppies, daisies, and weeds.
Reaching for colors that caught her eyes.
Petal by petal, one by one, she loves him, she loves him not.
At the end of her last petal, she regathered herself, took a deep breath, and sighed releasing carbon dioxide into the air

Wondering if she should make a wish or just
allow the petal to blow into the breeze
It was in that moment she realized the purpose
of their chaotic relationship
She learned how to speak up.
He accepted that it was time for him to own up.
With that epiphany, she stood up, laid the petal
on the ground, and walked away.

I can breathe
I can inhale and exhale
I can see
I can feel
I can touch
This is wonderful
Thank God this is real

*-That moment you realize you can do whatever
you want, and there's no stopping you*

Me vs Me

Loving me.
Starting over.
New love.
Fresh love.
I'm not the same person 2 to 3 years ago.
I'm in a new environment.
I see new surroundings.
How do I love me where I am?
Do I go back to the familiar?
Or, do I try something new?
I am ready to let go to become the person I'm
meant to be for me and no one else.

Love Starts With Me

How do I start to love me?
Do I hug myself?
Do I kiss my hand?
That's the thing.
Love isn't physical.
It's mental.
It's expressive.
How you love yourself will show.
How you love others will show.
How you allow others to love you will show.

-Love is not what it says, but what it does.

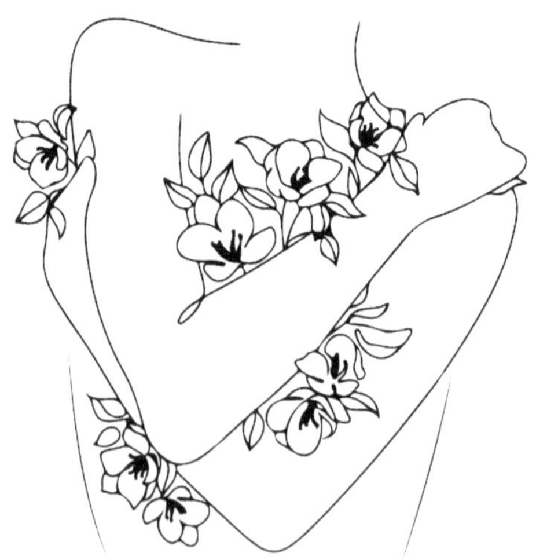

Inner Me

Letting go
Finally letting go
Breathing, inhaling, exhaling
Accepting, hearing from God
Sitting in silence, deleting
No more wondering what ifs
Accept the protection and the grace
I will produce new oil
This requires a new process
A different type of crushing
This is extra special
A true gift from God
I've shown compassion through prayer
There's nothing left for me to do
But move forward into what
God is calling me to do
I ask that you watch over me
In fact, come on this journey with me
I would love to share it with you.
You can be my inner me.

The Darkness

Stagnantly Moving

Moving on is tough.
Moving on can be difficult.
Moving on becomes the bridge to better days
and evolving reality.
Moving on creates new memories.

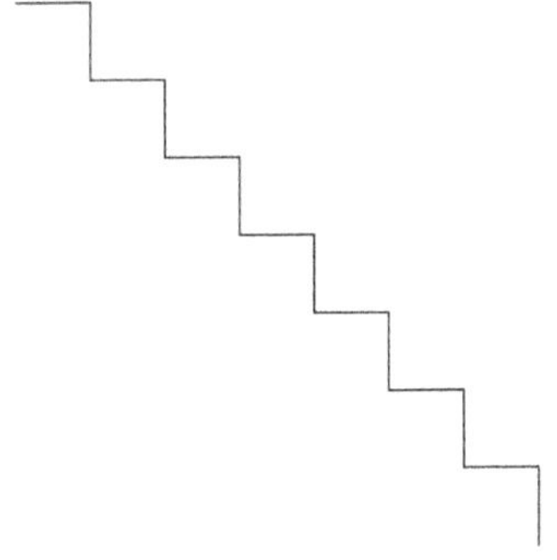

It took me months to genuinely smile again
I forgot my mouth could curve upwards
That's when the pain slowly started to melt
away.

-Smile, it's free therapy

I love you
Always will
My love was
Never fake
I was there
To help you
Heal.

-Don't force yourself onto someone, if they see you, they see you

I wanted love from you so much
That I refused to allow my eyes
To see the real vision.

-Take off the sunglasses and put on the prescription eyeglasses, they were advised for a reason

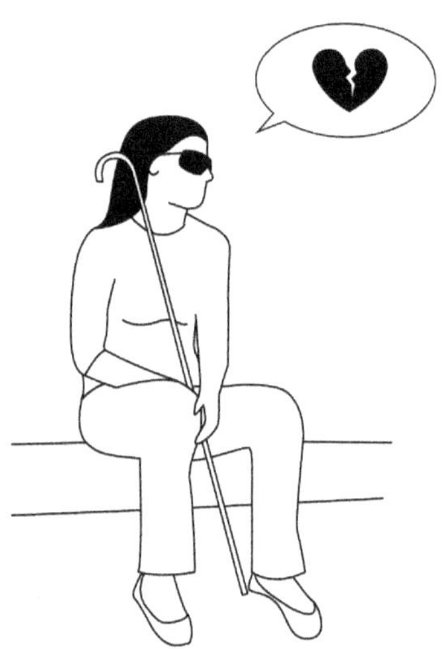

The thorn stuck in my side was agonizing and
painful
I wanted God to remove it
Instead, God allowed me to endure it and use it
For His Glory and for my story.

*-Never despise the challenging and tough
storms, the sun will shine again with an
occasional rainbow*

When you love so deep
You'll do anything to work it out
Even at the sake of your own sane mentality
When you know in fact it's time for you to
Get out.

-Trust your intuition, it's your spirit talking to you

The truth hurts so bad
That I'd rather
Believe the lies.

-*Truth is there to warn, not hurt*

-*Lies are there to avoid, not provide freedom*

One year the mask slipped
That year I witnessed it
The next year I accepted it.

*-Believe a person when they show you who they
are the first time*

The more I listen to you, the more I understand
you.
The more I listen to you, the more I don't
understand you.

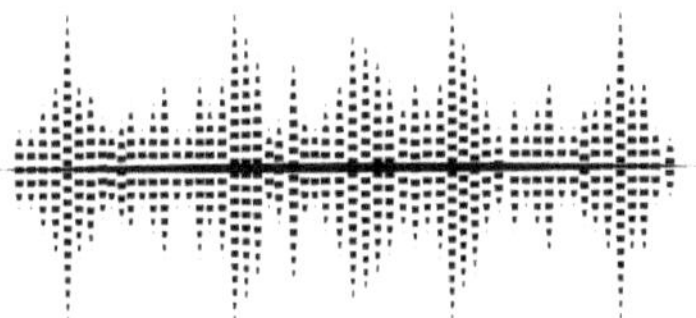

Who Sent You

I don't know what to think
Or how to think at this moment.
I don't know what's real
Or what's fake.
I don't know who sent you.

Missed Red Flags

Shit forever coming out the bag
When I look back, damn it's sad
How I was so naive
Thinking the other person could achieve
When to be honest
I was scared to leave
Wondering if love would come no more
This time it just came knocking at my door
With an empty glass
And nothing to pour.

Letter to myself, again

I get so confused about why I'm here.
Sometimes I can't decipher between God and
the enemy.
I'm clouded, confused with no sense of
direction. I thought I knew what I wanted for my
life, but I guess I don't.
This is tough on me mentally, physically,
emotionally, spiritually. Like, I really don't
know what to do.
Should I stay or go? Should I just run and give
up on everything? I'm so close to saying to hell
with it.
Not-so-pleasant thoughts have crossed my mind
several times. I feel like no one gets me,
understands me, or truly knows who I am.
I feel like people look to me for answers. I don't
know shit. I don't know if I'm coming or going.
Sometimes I just want to be left alone. No one
listens to me. I feel like I'm a prisoner to myself.

Questions for God

God, what is happening? I really don't know what to say or how to feel.
Is this really real? Like is it? I hope this is no hoax. But for what?
Honestly, I don't know how to feel. I'm just observing and trying my best to decipher what's taking place.
I don't know what to say or what to do.
I'm lost, at a standstill. How do I know if it's real? Am I just a fake? Could I be a failure?
Then my pen struggles with letters and consonants and vowels.
Is this really a gift or a distraction? I'm going to submit to Your will. What is the sacrifice to do Your will?
God, am I on the right path? Am I doing anything wrong? What decision should I make?
Speak to me, Lord. I need to hear from you. I need guidance. I'm thirsty for you God.

Letter to Myself

I literally feel stupid. I feel lost. I feel like I
don't know who I am or why I'm even here.
Why can't I take up for myself? Or stand up for
myself? Why do I feel like I'm being taken
advantage of?
Am I that desperate for love? Am I that naive?
Am I really ignoring the truth?
I feel like I'm slowly allowing myself to sink
into a dark place. This has been a complete
distraction from the very beginning.
I've been on edge from the very beginning. Yet,
I've ignored everything from the very beginning.
Then the things I ignore come back on me like it
was my fault, but I've been doing nothing.
Maybe that's the problem. I don't do nothing.
I'm tired of allowing the views of others to
control my life.
How do I start over from here? Where do I go?
Am I in too deep to pack up and go?
This is not what I envisioned.